Especially for

Joni

From

Kirsty

Date

12 | 2 | 24

ISBN 978-1-61626-928-9

Published by Barbour Publishing, Inc., P.O. Box 719, Uhrichsville, Ohio 44683, www.barbourbooks.com

Our mission is to publish and distribute inspirational products offering exceptional value and biblical encouragement to the masses.

Printed in China.
Leo Paper, Gulao Town, Heshan City, Guangdong, China; October 2012; D10003488

Life's Little Book
of Wisdom
for Girls

BARBOUR
PUBLISHING

Your eye color. . .your curly, straight, or wavy hair. . .your voice. . .these are things that make you different from anyone else on the planet— and all were chosen just for you by the Master Creator.

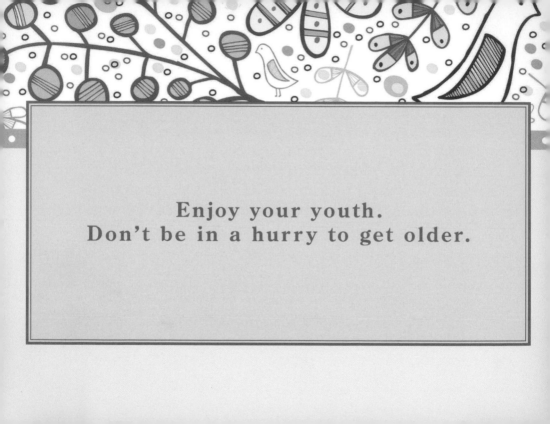

Enjoy your youth.
Don't be in a hurry to get older.

Be a good example.

Respect the ideas
and opinions of others
(even though you may not agree).

Return a harsh word
with a kind one.

On your worst days,
smile anyway.

Happy is the person who trusts the Lord.

PSALM 40:4 ICB

Always stand up for what's right.

Share God's love
with others.

Be fair.

Remember that appearances
can be deceiving.

Make the most of your
God-given talents.

JOANNE DECKER

Find a role model—a family member,
friend, or teacher. . . . It's helpful to
have someone to look up to and
who shares your interests.

YOLANDA CHUMNEY

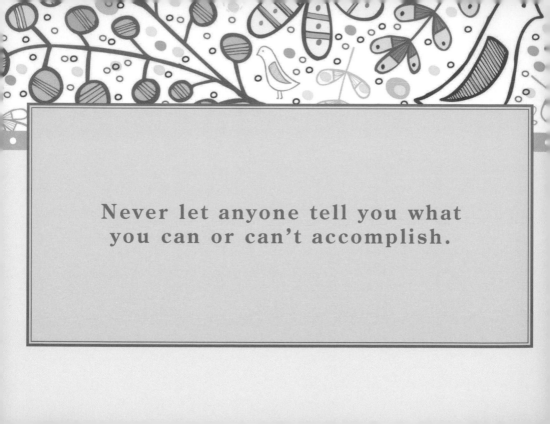

Never let anyone tell you what you can or can't accomplish.

Each day is an opportunity
to learn something new.

God has amazing
plans for your life.

Being modest doesn't
mean being out of style.

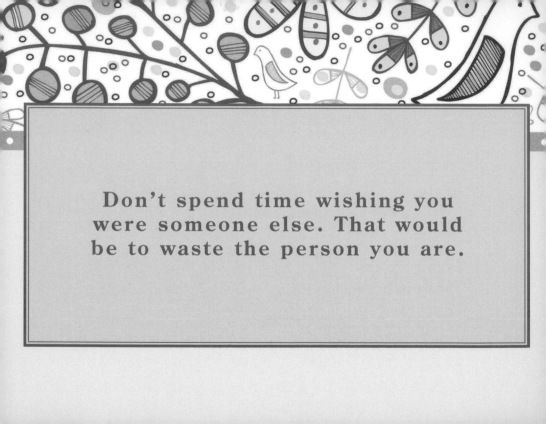

Don't spend time wishing you were someone else. That would be to waste the person you are.

God created you to be you and nobody else.

CONOVER SWOFFORD

The Lord. . .
delights in honesty.

PROVERBS 11:1 NLT

Be honest—
even when it's not
the easy thing to do.

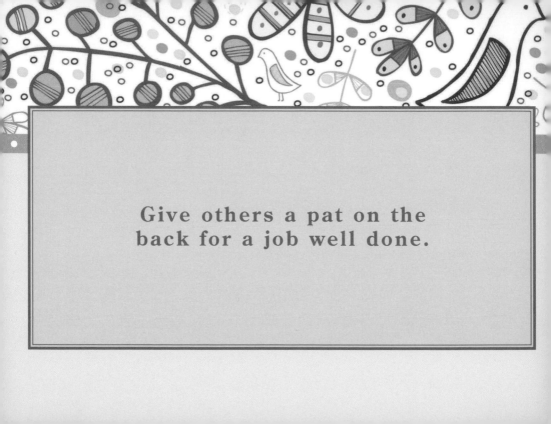

Give others a pat on the
back for a job well done.

Read God's Word.

Laugh with your friends.

Work hard, but always
make time for play.

Be considerate.

Hug your parents and tell them
how much you love them.

Believe in your heart that
God will do what He says—
because He always will!

Talk to God—you can trust
Him with anything.

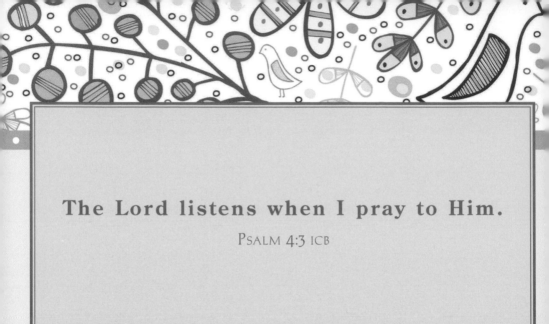

The Lord listens when I pray to Him.

PSALM 4:3 ICB

Ask questions.
You'll be amazed at what
you can learn.

Do the best you can with the
gifts God has given you.

If you have a sister,
make an effort to also be her friend.

When a friend acts
unlovable,
love her anyway.

You'll get a lot farther with
a "please" than a whine.

ANONYMOUS

Give more
than you get.

JOANNE DECKER

Don't borrow anything
without asking first.

Respect others.

Respect yourself.

Don't ever stop being kind. . . .
Let kindness and truth
show in all you do.

PROVERBS 3:3 ICB

**Be kind to your pets.
They're part of God's creation, too.**

VICKIE PHELPS

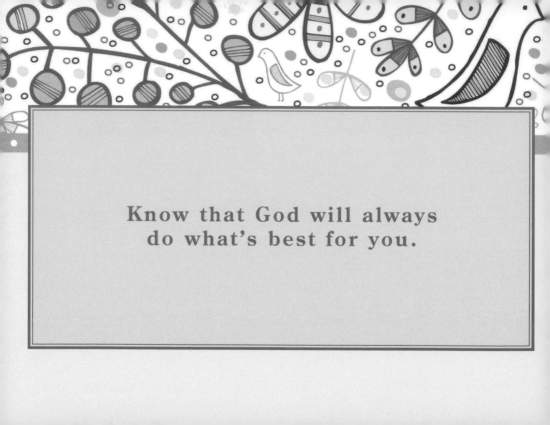

Know that God will always
do what's best for you.

Sometimes it's better to listen more than you talk.

Spend time with
your grandparents.
They can teach you a lot.

God created you—He made
you into the unique, beautiful,
and talented individual you are.

If you make a mess,
clean it up.

Just because you want
something doesn't mean
it's what you really need.

Show appreciation
to your teachers.

Be a good neighbor.

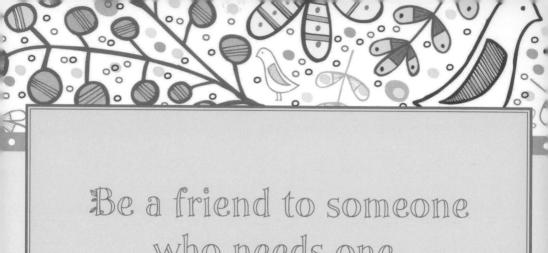

Be a friend to someone
who needs one.

No matter how bad today may be,
remember that you can start
over again tomorrow.

Choose not to
pass along gossip.

Be gentle and polite to all people.

TITUS 3:2 ICB

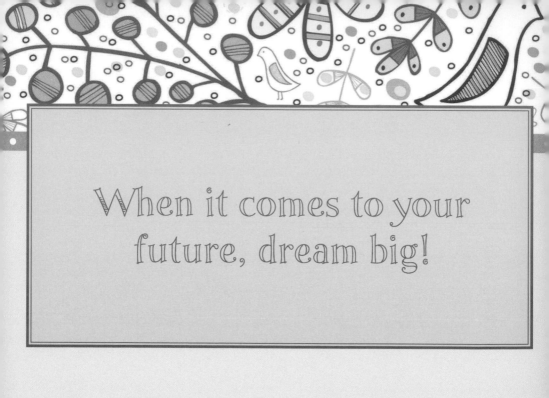

When it comes to your
future, dream big!

Be the best you that you can be.

If you fail, try again.

Learn from your mistakes.

Pray for others.

Boldly take action if you can make
a difference in someone's life.

Don't be too quick to dislike others.
You've never walked in their shoes.

Give a hug or an encouraging
word when someone needs it.

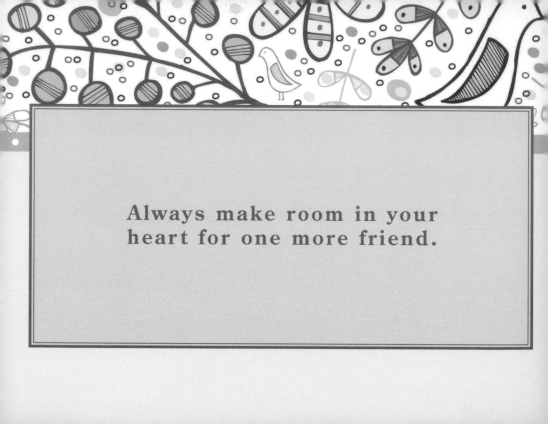

Always make room in your heart for one more friend.

Take turns.

True friends won't pressure
you to choose something
that isn't right for you.

YOLANDA CHUMNEY

A true friend cares
about your dreams, too.

The only way to have a friend is to be one.

RALPH WALDO EMERSON

When you're smiling on the inside, it shows on the outside.

BONNIE JENSEN

God knows just what you need—
even before you do.

If you need help,
don't be too proud to ask.

Share your happiness
with others.

The little things can make
a very big difference.

As a child of God, you're a princess in His kingdom.

Your relationship with Jesus
is very important to Him.

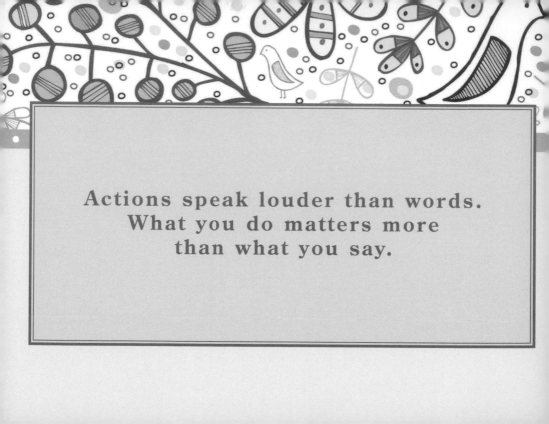

Actions speak louder than words.
What you do matters more
than what you say.

No matter what anyone says
about you. . .no matter what
they think about you. . .
you know the truth,
and that's all that matters.

Make an effort to get
along with others.

**Don't fight with your family—
there are plenty of other people in the
world to give you a hard time.**

ANONYMOUS

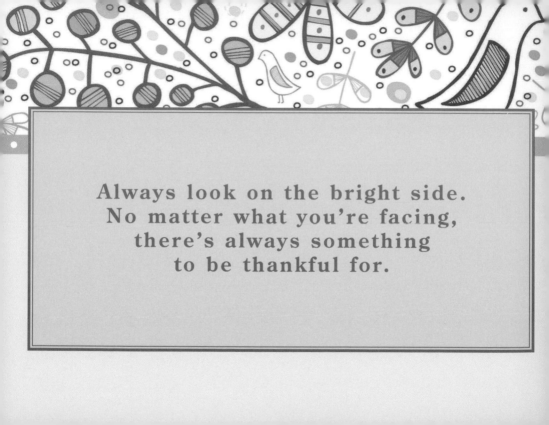

Always look on the bright side.
No matter what you're facing,
there's always something
to be thankful for.

Have the courage to say no.

JOANNE DECKER

The best friends to have are the
ones who bring out the best in you.

Don't get caught up
in the opinions of others.

Don't spend your time trying to get even with someone who has hurt you. Instead, forgive and turn it over to God.

Keep praying.
God will answer when
the time is right.

With God's help,
you can do anything!

You are my wonderful God
who gives me courage.

PSALM 3:3 ICB

Remember that sunshine always follows the rain.

Don't rush through the day too fast.
You never know what you might miss.

Nothing can separate you
from God's love and care.

It's nice to be important,
but it's more important to be nice.

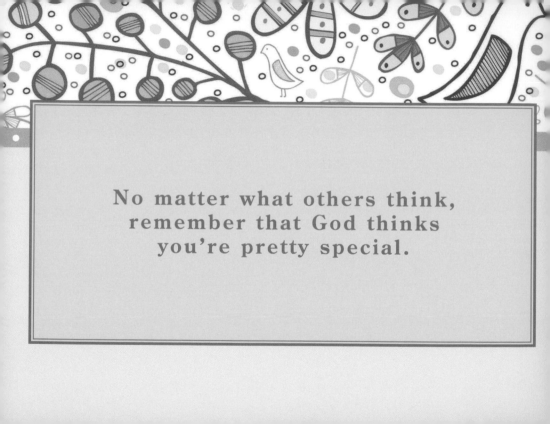

No matter what others think,
remember that God thinks
you're pretty special.

True beauty shines
from within.

Expect only the best
to happen every day.

Don't be afraid to make mistakes.
Mistakes are part of growing up.

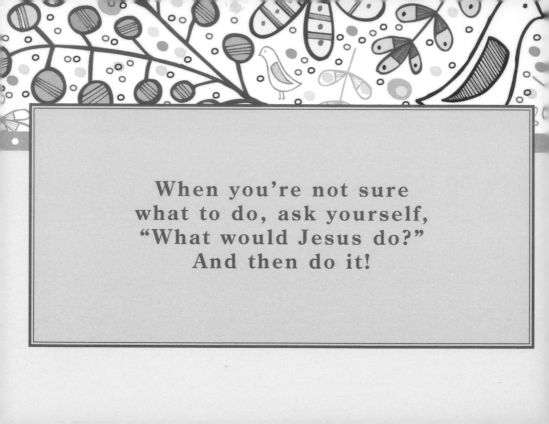

When you're not sure
what to do, ask yourself,
"What would Jesus do?"
And then do it!

It's not about how much you can give; it's about giving with a joyful heart.

Choose your friends wisely.
Your closest friends have the greatest
influence on your heart.

Partner with God,
and you can change
the world.

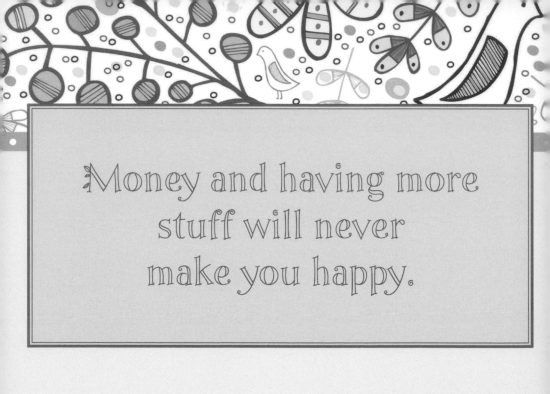

Money and having more
stuff will never
make you happy.

Don't let the world influence you to do
something that would make God sad.
Ask God for strength to make
the right decisions.

Whatever embarrassment you're facing
today will be forgotten tomorrow.

Serving others will
make you glad.

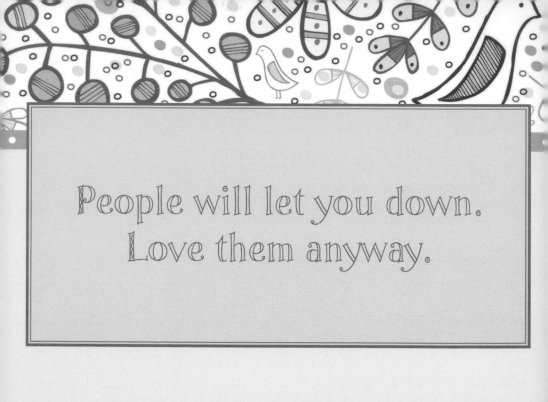

People will let you down.
Love them anyway.

Friends are important—
make as many as you can.

ANONYMOUS

Good friends are a sure way
to lots of happy memories.

Be yourself.
Don't waste time trying to
be like everyone else.

Think before you talk.

You can't hide
anything from God.

Ask God to make
you more like Him.

Be a good
listener.

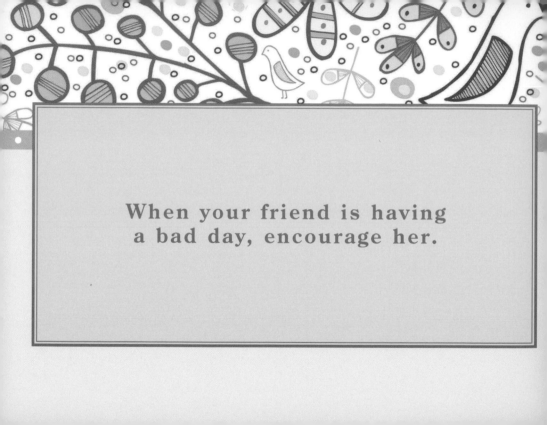

When your friend is having
a bad day, encourage her.

Begin and end each
day with a prayer.

You're never too young to
make a difference
in the world.

If you have a brother,
treat him well. Someday, you'll
want him to return the favor.

Always keep
your promises.

When you are weak,
God will make you strong.

Be happy with your
friends when they're happy.

Be sad with your friends when they're sad.

Enjoy today;
don't worry about
tomorrow.

A few things to cherish:
a trusted girlfriend. . .
and a good book.

BONNIE JENSEN

Jesus can handle any
problem that you face.

If you feel like no one understands you, remember that God does. He's your closest friend!

Some days will be hard—
just hang on!
It will get better.

Never say, "I can't. . . ,"
because you never know until you try.

Never give up.

When we mess up, God always
gives us a second chance.
All we have to do is ask.

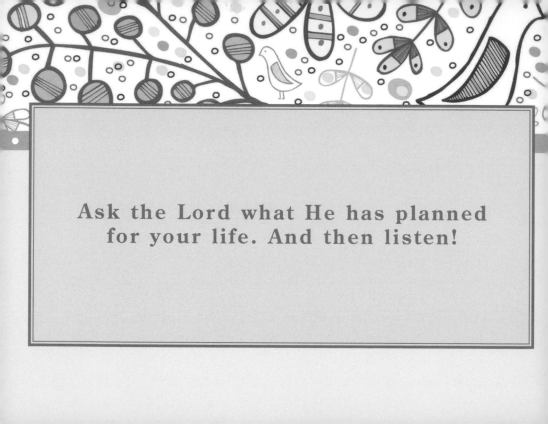

Ask the Lord what He has planned
for your life. And then listen!

People may not act like you think
they should. . .but love them anyway.

You don't have to be perfect.
God loves you right now—
just the way you are.

**The forgiveness you give
to others will be given to you.**

Matthew 7:2 icb

When someone hurts your feelings,
forgive them. . . .

And be quick to say "I'm sorry"
when you hurt someone else.

If you have a home, family, friends,
and food to eat. . .what more
could you want or need?

Make an effort to stop
a fight before it starts.

Stop trying to "fix" others—
and just love them.

Don't judge and don't blame.
Listen and care instead.

When you're worried, pray!
When you're lonely, pray!
When you're afraid, pray!
When you're joyful, pray!

Love is best of all. There is not,
nor ever shall there ever be,
true friendship without it.

UNKNOWN

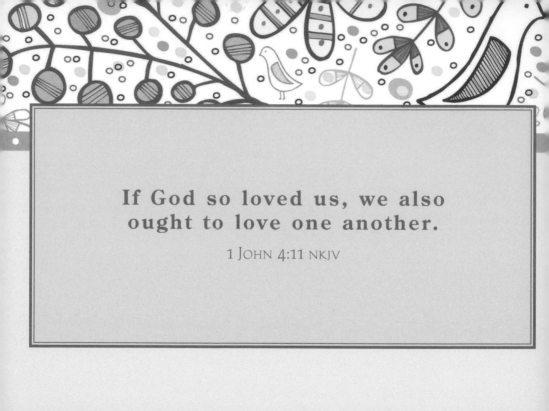

If God so loved us, we also ought to love one another.

1 JOHN 4:11 NKJV

Even when you're super busy,
make time for your friends.

You don't have to do anything special to earn God's love. He already loves you just the way you are!

When you're unsure about something,
God's Word will tell you
exactly what to do.

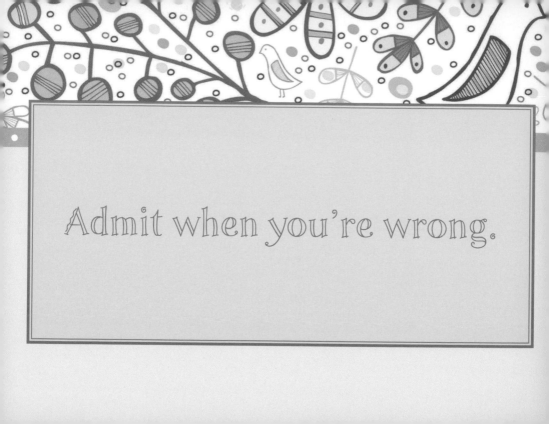

Admit when you're wrong.

Say only nice things about others.

A little work never killed anyone.

ANONYMOUS

Thank your parents
for all they do for you.

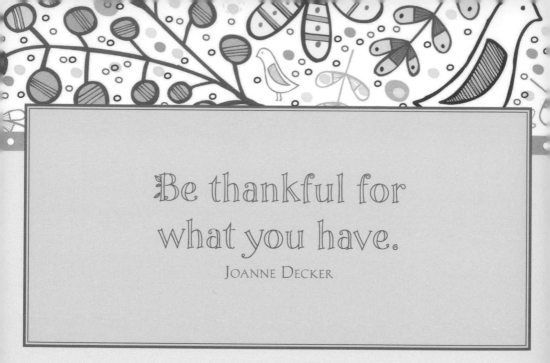

Be thankful for
what you have.

JOANNE DECKER

Say "thank You" to God for making
the earth and everything in it.

God is good. . .all the time!

**The best way to cheer yourself up
is to cheer somebody else up.**

Mark Twain

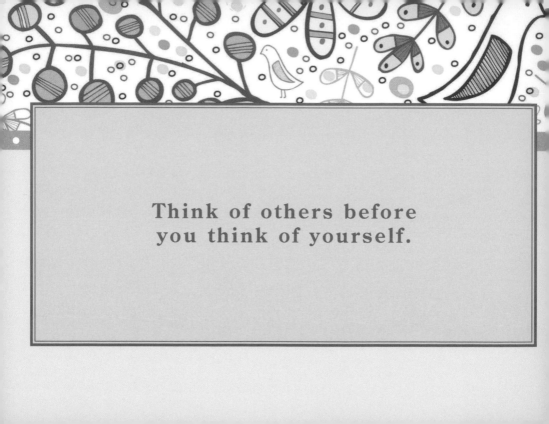

Think of others before
you think of yourself.

Pass on the kindnesses
others show you.

Be an encouragement to others.
Sometimes even one word is enough.

Encourage someone
else's dreams.

Appreciate the differences between yourself and others.